William H. Matchett
London
April, 1981

The Phoenix Living Poets

<hr>

WATER VOICES

AF333593

Poets Published in
The Phoenix Living Poets Series

*

JAMES AITCHISON
GEORGE MACKAY BROWN
MICHAEL BURN · PHILIP CALLOW
ROBERT CONQUEST · JOHN COTTON
GLORIA EVANS DAVIES
PATRIC DICKINSON
D.J. ENRIGHT
JOHN FULLER
J.C. HALL · MOLLY HOLDEN
P.J. KAVANAGH
CHRISTOPHER LEVENSON
EDWARD LOWBURY · NORMAN MacCAIG
DIANA McLOGHLEN
JAMES MERRILL
LESLIE NORRIS · RICHARD OUTRAM
RODNEY PYBUS
ADRIENNE RICH · ANNE SEXTON · JON SILKIN
JON STALLWORTHY
EDWARD STOREY · TERENCE TILLER

WATER VOICES

By

LESLIE NORRIS

CHATTO AND WINDUS

THE HOGARTH PRESS

1980

Published by
Chatto and Windus Ltd
with The Hogarth Press Ltd
40 William IV Street
London WC2 4DF

*

Clarke, Irwin & Co Ltd
Toronto

All rights reserved. No part of this publication may be reproduced, stored in a retrieval system or transmitted in any form, or by any means, electronic, mechanical, photocopying, recording or otherwise, without the prior permission of Chatto and Windus Ltd.

British Library Cataloguing in Publication Data
Norris, Leslie
   Water voices. — (Phoenix living poets).
   I. Title II. Series
   821'.9'14   PR6027.044A17
   ISBN 0-7011-2518-7

© Leslie Norris 1980

Printed in Great Britain by
Redwood Burn Ltd
Trowbridge & Esher

For Robert Manning

Acknowledgements

Some of these poems have appeared in *The Atlantic Monthly, The Anglo-Welsh Review, Delta, Limestone, The London Magazine, The New Statesman, The New Yorker, PEN New Poems 1973–1974, 1976–1977, Poetry Northwest, Poetry Wales, The Scotsman* and *The Poetry Book Society Supplement* for Christmas '75. Thanks are due also to the BBC, ITV, The Globe Playhouse Trust, The South-East Arts Association, *Poetry Dimension* and The Tidal Press, Maine.

'At The Sea's Edge in Pembrokeshire' was commissioned for the 900th Anniversary Celebrations of Winchester Cathedral.

Contents

WATER VOICES

Christmas Day

Winter drought, and a parched wind
Roughens the mud. Wrapped in a parka,
Leaning bleakly into the slack
The blast misses as it screams over

The blackthorn, I'm tramping a
Chalk ditch from the downs. Leaves
Dry as cornflakes crack under
My gumboots, the hedge is against

My shoulder. Sands of their flying
Dusts hunt the spent fields, ice
Grains stick at my eyes. Caught
On the thorns, a rip of newsprint

Shivers its yellow edges, grows
Long, then rises easily, a narrow
Heron, out of shadow. It rises,
Trailing its thin legs, into cold

Sun flat as the land. Upright,
Broad wings spread, neck curved
And head and great blade turned
Down on the lit breast, it hangs

Against barbs, against winter
Darkness, before its slow vanes
Beat once over the elms, a
Christ crucified, a flying Christ.

Lear at Fifty

This morning early, driving the lanes in my
    Glib metal, frost fur on the brambles,
The grass, the hasps and bars of gates, first
    Sun burning it away in clinging wisps,
I saw an old man, sweeping leaves together, outside
    The Black Horse. His face held night's

Stupor, the lines of his age had not stiffened
    Against the daylight. He shifted his
Feet to careful standing, and then his broom,
    His necessary crutch, moved like an
Insect on slow, frail, crawling legs from
    Leaf to leaf. The small gusts of

My passing broke his labour, heaps of the dry
    Work spilling and flying. Nobody
Walked on the shore. Waves, unexpected heavy waves
    From some wild, piling storm away at sea,
Ripped the mild sand, smashed rocks, and shot the
    Squalling gulls out of the filth, vomit

And glittering sewage the flung birds flocked for.
    And truly, the tide was high this morning;
Old shoes, cans, cynical gouts of accidental oil,
    Plastic bottles, ropes, bubbling detergent
Slime, all were thrown to the sea wall. I have
    No wish to remember those unwelcoming

Waves I turned my back on, nor to think of old men
    Sitting tight in their skulls, aghast
At what their soft, insistent mouths will keep on
    Yelling. But through the limpet hours
I've walked the fields as if on a cliff's edge,
    The idea of flight in me, and seen my

Friends, myself, all strong, governing men, turned
    Sticks, turned tottering old fools.
The last sun in its blaze brings yellow light
    To everything, walls, windows, water;
A false warmth. In the morning some old man will start
    To sweep his leaves to a neatness.

i.m. James Chuang, MB, BS, MRCS, RN
died April 23 1978, aged 25

Last Thursday morning, watching a haul of barges
tug their blunt ropes under Chelsea Bridge,
I saw two swallows, hot from Africa,
flick and scream across the delighted river.
First of the warming year, emblem and omen,
one for each day of all that remained of your life.

Jim, I can't understand how anyone as young
and generous could go so swiftly into death.
It was good that afternoon, walking in Hyde Park,
watching the little goldeneye, pair by pair
in meticulous black and white, bobbing
on the cold Serpentine. To see them dive!

They'd slip under the water so casually,
without taking breath, without preparation
slide into the silence, longer and deeper,
until we couldn't see them. They all came back.
One by one all popped up from their underworld,
out of their darkness. Small London children,

playing with grandparents, clapped their hands
at each abrupt return. We spoke of your work
at Greenwich Hospital, the Seamen's Hospital
down by the widening Thames, and I was startled
by the wholeness of your compassion, your serious
tolerance. You were a chosen man. Somewhere

away from my awareness you had come of age.
And since then I've been finding it difficult
to remember you as a small boy, that brush-head,
the apricot-coloured child who would bring his
reading book, or that older one in Christ's
Hospital blue, alert, smiling, always eager.

On Thursday afternoon I knew you the full man,
conscious of healing, able to keep death at bay
down there near the river. Images of your childhood
were not wanted. You had become my contemporary,
although you were young enough to clap your hands
with the children, and I stand in an older body.

(Conscious of certain wreck, Jim, I had meant
to ask about arthritis, how my fingers stiffen;
but had not thought to know the pain of knocking
these words out.) To think a starling's nest,
untidy tangle of instinct pressed messily
into an air vent, could have killed you.

Anger meant little to you. If I am angry
it is a futility you must allow me now.
Two Canada geese, those heavy winter birds,
grey on a grey sky, beat overhead, trailing
silence behind their ponderous flying.
A cold evening has come back to the country.

Ponies

Stepping delicately, the ponies, the palominos,
Yellower than cream, smooth as butter, as bright
As the swags of ragwort they step among.

Stones in the river Brân, rounded as bubbles,
Limestone and sandstone tumbled from Fwng and Cedny,
And brilliant shallow water over them.

Heavy over the viaduct the belligerent engine,
Imminent, cloudless thunder beneath the arches,
A young man's tombstone under the hollow echo.

> *A white rose, his quiet life*
> *Fell in quiet to his grave.*
> *Quiet now, without a breeze,*
> *He sleeps in quiet, sleeps in peace.*

Unmoving, in an old darkness near the river,
The inquisitive ponies, the mild palominos,
Standing among hawthorns, snags of wild roses.

Lines For The Bastard Prince

His father's empty coffin, chipped
from the stone with a driven chisel
to keep the old man cold. Here spread
his hollow shoulders, and there

his ankle-bones were clipped. The air
and powder of those flying bones are lost.
But the boy's different. A blunt middle-weight,
balanced, powerful, such energy's even about

his rest his effigy can scarcely hold him in.
Oh, he was a tough one, neat and brutal
in attack, with a fast counter. His mother
was a fresh girl from the villages, her

blood could not expect the honour
of a cut tomb in the chapel, she did not
earn for her feet a carved dog, symbol
of fidelity. This firm prince is her memorial.

At The Sea's Edge,
In Pembrokeshire

Peter de Leia, dead eight
hundred years, began this
structure. Not having the
saint's art, nor learned
his psalter from a gold-
beaked pigeon, he built
in common stone. He exalted
labour into a stone praise.

Nor was he baptised in live
waters conveniently burst
forth to supply the shaken
drops for that ceremony. To
reach his pulpit he climbed
a joiner's steps, did not expect
the ground to lift in a sudden
hillock so that he could preach
in open piety to the rapt Welsh.

When he laid down the square-
ended presbytery, with aisles,
transepts, tower and nave, he saw
his masons bleed if the chisel
slipped. One fell in his sight
from the brittle scaffolding
and the two legs snapped
audibly, hitting the ground.
He had not the saint's skill

to stop that falling which must
fall. Such clear faith was not
possible, the rule of the world
grown strong. He knew that right
building was a moral force, that
stone can grow. An earthquake

has tested this cathedral. In
Pembrokeshire, near the saint's
river, at the edge of the sea,

de Leia built well, saw stone
vault and flower. A plain man,
building in faith where God
had touched the saint, he saw
the miracle which is not swift
visitation, nor an incredible
suspension of the commonplace,
but the church grown great about us,
as if the first stone were a seed.

Once Upon A Time

There was this little birch tree
And they said she should have leaves
By mid-May.
She could have danced, almost,
For that promise
And because she was as skinny as a child.

But first, they said, there would come
A warm wind; and he did.
He teased her, he waltzed her around, she was
Dizzy and sweet and tender
In every bud.
And when the bird came
And sat on a thin twig
Singing, Now, it's Now —

She didn't understand at all,
Not at all.
But in the evening
She stood slender and gowned
In her freshness, her translucent new green,
And she was absolutely transformed.

She turned about slowly,
Loosening herself quite free of dirt.
Ho hum, she sang, very quietly, now
To sail, like a green veil, over the hill,
For ever, away for ever
— Said the little birch tree.

(from the Norwegian of Tarjei Vesaas)

Unchanging

Every seven years, is it, the body's
Changed? Flake by dry flake the skin
Renewed, glands and muscles altered
Secretly in their smooth liquids?
Hair, nails, how we shear them away,
Slow modifications unnoticed almost,
Until one day an accident of the mirror
Shows the remade man, grown different

Silently. All's changed then; eyes,
Manipulation of the senses, the very
Instruments of love are changed. The world's
Grown calcinous. What miracle, when
That which we call the heart is still
Immutable constancy, unchanged love.

Moonman

Last night I walked under the moon,
One of its green shadows, my eyes
A reflection of the chill moon.

Rounder than harvest, more cold
Than remembered frost, it burned
With sterile ardour the skin

Of the lane I walked. I know
It will be diminished, pared
Crescent recognisably, but say

It must grow again in its due time
More coldly blazing for the sleek
Ice to come. I had not thought

How I, too, wane as you turn away
Your sunlight, am great only
In harvests of your love.

Cave Paintings

i   After Dark

After dark, police sirens rip us
Awake. We crouch, hands over ears, our walls
Too small to hold such raucous invasion.

In Woodland Park, in caves
Of municipal concrete, the wolf
Shivers, the cougar shakes her chained ears.

ii   A Dish of Pebbles

Pebbles in a dish: opal, jade,
And one against sufficient light
A palpable smoke. All these

Are from Californian beaches. But here's
From Oregon a stone, from the castellated
Rim of the continent, its moats holding

Sea lions, voices of moist caves. Spray
Decorates the sky, the rattle of draining
Pebbles runs south from river-mouth to river-

Mouth. Here are sharks' teeth, two, for
Needling, bloodletting. And I have arrowheads:
This, from Washington; that, of greater age, from Somerset.

iii   A Thrush

The thrush comes into the house, I hear
Its soft battering against the window glass.

And I leave my desk, speaking to it,
Tolerate its panic, its round, wild eye,

The way it spreads its wings in a bare
Ache against the pane. I am accustomed

To creatures, release it. It leaves behind
Two slight feathers, the yellow stain of its droppings.

iv   Ancestor

There is no photograph, but I think him
Tall. He stood in twenty acres of grass
And a whole unfenced mountain uprose

Behind him. Certainly he worked
Eight sons timid, ruled all daylight,
Roaring at animals. Left, at the end,

Nothing, but was the last of us, long
Ago, to come off that brutal soil with
Innocent power. So I think him tall.

24

v   In Still Clay

A Staffordshire greyhound, fawn, couchant,
Thin, stylised neck and flexible white hocks,
He sits in still clay on a dais of royal blue.

Six inches in length, the glaze crazed
Nowhere, and one gold line untarnished
Along the hollow plinth, he is preserved

By lucky accident. Pharoahs knew his like.
He dreams in the shadow between two shelves,
Linking time with time. Is a potent hunter.

vi   Scatterings of Light

Waterfalls, pools, streams, rivers,
And the loud, monotonous, empty

Drop through the centuries; the cave
Remembers water, was drilled

By water. Scatterings
Of light floated among bats

Pendulous as fruit in the rock's
Cold branches. A dry cave holds

Darkness to its walls, as water
Holds the shape of its flowing.

vii   Paperweight

This domed, heavy glass, it satisfies
The hand. Its concentric flowers, whorls,

Shells and coloured rods, its airy
Bubbles even, all are held in a still

Dance. I keep it for its solid
Roundness against time, and for the men,

In France two hundred years ago, who by
Some perfect means of their mortality

Made it, full and heavy, from fragile silicas,
And sent its casual permanence to my hand.

viii   Symbols

Emblems, plaques, icons, symbols
Of the decaying hand; stones, or

Feathers, identified by warm
Sight, and touched, and put

Aside; or voices,
Transferred as they vanish

In handled syllables, we keep
From the breaking dust, against

The filling of the cave. For
The cave is filling, fills

Rapidly. It closes,
From the eyes in.

Grooming

The poem stands on its firm
legs. Its claws are filed, brush
and curry-comb have worked
with the hissing groom to polish

its smooth pelt. All morning, hair
by hair, I've plucked away each small
excess; remains no trace of
barbering, and all feels natural.

It is conditioned to walk, turn
to the frailest leash, swing
without effort into ecstatic
hunting. Now I am cleaning

the teeth in its lion jaws
with an old brush. I'll set it
wild on the running street, aimed
at the hamstring, the soft throat.

Hyperion

was hardly a Titan. He stood
a brief inch over six feet, was
sweetly made. Not for his size
am I sent in his just praise
along the measured tracks

of his achievement. Dropped
on the printed turf by Selene,
daughter of Serenissima, he moved
even in his first uncertainty
like one waited for. His birth

was in green April, and he grew
in light, on the fat meadows.
Gently schooled, he delighted
his mentors with his perfect ardour,
honesty, the speed of his response.

Though small, he was quite beautiful,
his chestnut mane burning, his step
luminous. Some doubted his courage,
looking askance at the delicacy
of his white feet, ignoring the star

already brilliant in his forehead.
His heart was a vivid instrument
drumming for victory, loin and muscle
could stretch and flex in eating
leaps. When he ran, when he ran

the rings of his nostrils were scarlet,
the white foam spun away from his lips.
For his was the old, true blood,
untainted in his veins' walls:
two lines to St. Simon, two lines

to Bend Or: The Flying Dutchman,
Bayardo, Galopin, all the great ones
back in his pedigree met in him.
He could not fail to honour
his fathers in the proud flood

of his winning. Nine times he left
his crescent grooves in the cheering
grass before the commoners gasped
after him. At Epsom, racing as if
alone on the classic track, he won

a record Derby, at Doncaster the Leger.
He won the Chester Vase, the Prince
of Wales's Stakes. Nor in his fullness,
drowsing in quiet fields in quiet company,
was he forgotten. His children,

sons and daughters of the Sun,
did not allow this. Hypericum,
Sun Chariot, Rising Light, all
were his. And Sun Stream, Midas,
Owen Tudor, Suncastle, many others.

The swift Godiva was his, and in
his image famous Citation, who ran
away with all America. Sportsmen,
all who go to the races, who marvel
at the flying hooves, remember Hyperion.

Ormonde

The great Ormonde was a roarer —
unsound in wind: but was never beaten.

The loud blemish of his flesh
suggests mortality, that he was

to be reached by some pretender.
It was a deceitful flaw. The horse

was perfect. Winning the Guineas,
'he took despotic command, sped

forward, galloped over everything,
won cantering.' So John Porter

of Kingsclere, his trainer, exulting.
Carrying unjust weight, he was ridden,

by Archer often, to extravagant wins
in great events, was led in his fame

over the Thames to Park Lane, where all,
at their champagne, were delighted

by his charm, his grave manners. He ate
his sugar from ladies' gloved fingers

and went amiably home. After which
the ingrate Duke of Westminster sold him;

sold to the Argentine his greatness, the
one Ormonde. His few offspring never

lived up to him. How could they,
measured against perfection, do other

than disappoint? Even in age, tendons
inflexible as bone, blunt clubs

too far from his thinning blood to sense
the turf, he would not be defeated.

I have to think that natural death
stood off in awe and would not take

the match on level terms. A bullet
killed him, smacking into his skull

before the old horse truly knew
he was under orders. As well he was

unprepared. He would have outrun death.

**The beautiful young Devon Shorthorn Bull,
Sexton Hyades 33rd**

In warm meadows this bull
Ripens gently. He is a pod
Of milky seed, not ready yet.
Not liking to be alone, he
Drifts on neat feet to be near
His herd, is sad at gates
When one is taken from him. There's
No red in his eye, he does not
Know he's strong, but mildly

Pushes down hedges, can carry
A fence unnoticed on his broad
Skull. His flat back measures
The horizon. Get a ladder, look
Over him. Dream that, one by one,
The far fields fill with his children, his soft daughters.

Eagle and Hummingbird

Demure water, soft summer water,
Its rolling boulders dropped, its carried logs
Cast white as salt upon some resting beach,
I throw my spinners here, those small, beaked suns
Turning through steelheads, cut-throat, and the
Five-pound salmon come from the sea too young
Along the green channel of their instinct.

I stand midstream on rock, its roots in water,
Using the air to fly my singing line,
The burning spindle drifting through the river,
The river alders burning in the sun;
United elements, the one forgiving world
In whose veined heart I stand in a blue morning
Beneath the flash of hummingbirds, the smoulder

Of fishing eagles. Water and sun, fire
And reflected fire, the hundred suns
The river's mirror carries under the trees,
Buoyancy of the light birds, all's here,
All, all is here. And my thin line holds now
The lure of the hummingbird, its spinning
Breast, and the hooked voice of the eagle.

Ravenna Bridge

Thinking he walked on air, he
Thrust each step, stretched straight
His ankle. We saw him lift
On thinnest stone between him-
self and earth, and then dip on.

Such undulant progress! Stern
Herons walk like that; but he
Just rose again into his
Highest possible smiling air,
Stepped seriously by us,

And kept for all himself
The edges, even, of his happiness.
Passing, we caught the recognition
Of his transfiguring sweet
Smoke. And so he stepped, he

Skipped, the thin boy, on narrow
Ravenna Bridge, itself a height
Over pines and sycamores. He
Danced above their heads. If
He'd hopped the handrail, had

Swayed into flight, fallen
To stony death among wood-doves,
We should have watched him. I did
Not stand as I felt, hand
To mouth in a still gasp, but

Coldly and relaxed, and saw the boy
Perform his happy legs across
Ravenna Bridge and up the hill
To Fifty-Second. We walked home,
Thanking his god, and ours.

Marymere Falls

At the lip of the falls, small
Ferns totter in green air, tilt,
Lodge in a light pushed sideways,
As water, its level lost, pauses,

Grows heavy, and throws its slow
Roar outward, and down. Spray
Frets the marginal fall, imprisons
Sunlight in thin screens, climbs,

So frail its grains, against
All reasonable falling. But
Arc's full centre, its glistening
Plummet, profoundly falls, and falls

In booming pools, scatters,
Claps its steady diving over
Running stones, its words the poem's
Words: splash, rainbow, thunder.

A Reading in Seattle

Cold snow covers the summer
Mountains; they do not reject it.
Seas towed from Asia, immense
Pacific waters, invade the bays,
Roll heavy the long coast, turn
With a shake of the spray
And splinter the bleached
Lumber, sieve the lion-
Coloured sand. Inland, with
Lakes and the tamed
Salt of the Sound, is the lovely
City, safe in its washed air,
Holding its bridges calmly,
Its trees and tended grass,
The welcome of its wooden
Houses. At night, many
Lamps glitter cleanly, form
Stars in reflecting water
By skittering winds disturbed,
By small boats softly home
From fishing. The people sleep
In a ring of Japanese hills.
A hundred miles away a cone-
Shaped mountain measures the light.

Rivers, the rivers too.
Drop by plain drop they fall
From the cracking glaciers,
Collect in forming channels,
Roar, released, torrent of jade,
Opalescent fluid jewel,
Route of the salmon's instinct.
I stood once at the Skagit's edge
On a hot day, my face burned,
And walked slowly in, one step,
And another step, until I was

Waist deep in green flowing,
One with it, with the water.
Driving away through the little
Homesteads I was bereft. No man
Stands twice in the same river.

In the evening I thought
Of Dylan, how he had read
In Seattle. "The little slob,"
My friend said, marvelling,
"He read Eliot so beautifully,
Jesus, I cried." I did not answer.
In the city now the bars are
Empty of his stories
And only the downtown Indians
Are drunk as his memory.

I read in a hall full
Of friends, students, serious
Listeners. The great dead
Had spoken there, Auden,
Roethke, Watkins, many others.
There was room for a plump ghost.
I thought I heard his voice
Everywhere, after twenty years
Of famous death. The party over,
I walked home, saw on peaks
The coldest snow, white as bone.

Belonging

He came after the reading, when all
Had left, the students, the kind
Congratulating friends, and I was tired.

What it was gave me more than a
Public courtesy for this old man,
Small, neat in his blue suit, someone's

Grandfather, I can't say. He held
A paper faded as his eyes; his family
Tree. Anxious, erect, expecting my

Approval, he stood in the hot room.
"I'm Welsh," he said. I read his
Pedigree. Bentley, Lawrence, Faulkner,

Graydon, no Welsh names. I nodded,
Gave back his folded pride, shook
My head in serious admiration. Belonging,

After all, is mostly matter of belief.
"I should have known you anywhere," I said,
"For a Welshman." He put away his chart,

Shook hands, walked into the foreign light.
I watched him go. Outside, the sprinklers,
Waving their spraying rainbows, kept America green.

Islands off Maine
(for Charles and Jeannie Wadsworth)

1.
One man hammering
From his home on crevices
Shatters the darkness
Over the islands.

Dawn moves briskly
Among the rugosas
And the harbour lights take back
Their shaken images.

Water smooth as claws
Holds its silent traps;
On the visible tide
Floats huge America.

2.
In the spring of the year eight ospreys
Flew over the island; smaller birds
Squalled at them, pollack and mackerel
Spun in their flustered shoals beneath

The seahawks' wings. Six flew on
To cull more northern waters; two stayed,
Perched much on trees, and hunted
Entirely in flight, circling. Hung

Two hundred feet above what fish
They chose; and fell, the vertical
Steep plunge between their own
Talons, then the consummate grab.

For surface fish they disturbed
No more than the sea's lace before
Flicking away water and taking off,
But can dive a yard into the packed

Ocean, feet braced thick against impact,
The toes lined with spicules, the claws
Stiff, and the whole battered water suddenly
Over their five-foot wings. They close

Their nostrils against the salt entry
And never fail. A sodden flap off
The surface they shiver away droplets,
Carry their fish head first, a torpedo.

All summer we saw their young in the
Flattened spruce top, all day we heard
Their mewling hunger, until they flew
On the cooling air, down the long coast.

3.
And on the point one day,
Mist flattening the island,
I met the mad boy.

Brambles had torn his jeans,
His fingers were harsh as carrots,
Waterbeads dropped in his bull's curls.

His voice would not behave,
His skull was echoing and
The mist was behind his eyes.

"What d'you like about Maine,
Hey, what d'you like about it?"
Screaming like a blue jay.

Mountains, I told him, mostly
The mountains, but the sea too.
His joy was terrible, he hopped

In the gritty pebbles, he slapped
His laughing over the vague beach.
"Sure, there were mountains Monday

—today there ain't mountains!"
The island stopped where he pointed,
His hand wiped out Mount Cadillac.

"When you leaving, why don't you?
Why don't you leave? If you knew
The people here, you'd leave today!"

He moved away, was a stone, a
Post, a shape among shifting
Shapes, a slow uncertainty.

Unseen gulls jeered from the rocks.
Pewter light off the water
Faded when I hit the dirt path.

4.
Pink Harding, born on the island,
Counts time in decades. Her chair
Rocks away anything smaller.

In all her years the sea has not stopped
Running. Each tide piles higher the granite
Pebbles, the red granite and the grey.

Hummingbirds visit her white phlox.
She is glad to hear this, but has seen
Them before. She is up since dawn.

We shout down her deafness, but scar tissue
Rubs at her eyes. She no longer braids
The tied rugs for which she's famous.

"Some I had ten dollars for!" she still
Marvels, "And not always the best ones."
They're heirlooms now, hang in museums.

She speaks of her father, that good man,
Then sits up, lifts one hand in pride,
"My grandfather was a full-blooded Englishman."

5.
Four white posts and a length of chain
Enclose the burial ground. Its stillness
Is twelve low headstones among the spruce.
You could walk past it, your head down

Against mosquitoes, and not see it.
Here lie the old, in the amplitude
And honour of their longevity: Capt.
Thos. Manchester, AE 92 yrs 3 mos;

Hannah, his Wife, AE 87 yrs 5 mos;
And nine others. But Gilman U. Stanley,
A boy, he sailed east and north
Out of Cranberry, past Novia Scotia,

In the temperate summer of 1861, watched
With his living eyes the Atlantic
Shake back the pack ice off Cape Breton.
All his life he'd seen harbour porpoise,

But now he called the finback whale,
The humpback whale, the minke and right
Whales as they rolled and mountained in their
Buoyant schools across the Cabot Strait.

Rich waters! O rich, destructive waters!
Working northward, never far from landfall,
They kept Anticosti to larboard, and Cape Whittle
And Little Mecatina Island; and saw on the right

The grave Newfoundland headlands where they
Should be, reaching on June 16 the Strait
Of Belle Isle. Where the boy at once went
Down. The sea took him, pressed flat

His agile breath, swam him among rocks
In water blue as ice, broke him in deep
Currents so that he lolled boneless.
Son of Jonathan R. and Irene Stanley,

AE 16 yrs 8 mos 28 dys. Each year the scrub,
The quiet moss, the little evergreens, move
Like a slow green tide on his empty grave,
Break on his headstone, and the other headstones.

6.
water bell
    sea's angelus
        anchored edge of rock
and steep of water

        toll for us

audible hanging wave
    simple element
        mouth of the round tide
storm's voice

        toll for us
    in our leaving

water tongue
    clapper and safe hammer
        sea's elegy and sound

    celebrate our passing

        toll for us

In Maine, September

Soon now, storm windows
Will shutter the island houses.
The hummingbirds are flown,
The summer people travel south
Towards their warming dollars.
Pretty little sailboats,
Bouncing on trolleys,
Move into sheltered winters.

Its silvered bleaching
Adrift on summer grasses
And a tide of dandelions,
An old boat lies in quiet
Behind the long point.
Is an exhausted animal,
Its lines the whale's lines,
For bludgeoning, for cutting water.

Travelling West

March ends, and the wild month
Batters its last hours against the house.
Such driven rain, such a wind
Bellowing out of the west
Against the walls!
I sit in the late room,
Watch the curtains shiver, and think
Of the drenched counties of England,
Their shuddering pastures, the creaking fibres
Of oak and hanging beech.

The gutters are full, the uneasy road's
Awash; dazed cars buffet the flood
Behind their swimming headlights.
Perhaps the grey sea from the west
Has broken in at last, bringing
Its ancient flotsam, news
From the drowned islands, voices,
Branches of legendary trees.
But that old, distant coast
Will hold, it will hold always.

Although I saw it when the year
Had barely turned from summer,
The sea was snarling early,
Spun me as I swam, thrashed me
Among its grains with its upper hand,
Sank me in little storms.
Fighting for land, gasping,
Reeling, beaten deaf, I saw
The small farms in the hills
Light up their steady lamps.

Flew west over a sea spotted
With cloud, and three days later
Swam in kindlier water,

In Branch Lake, by the Penobscot River.
Had gone for togue and landlocked salmon,
But the sun lulled my hooks. I hung
In a hammock of water, warm silt soft
To the toes. Mallard
Feathered above my comfort, the long
Westering light streamed through the red oaks.

I have walked hard Pacific beaches,
Skin burned raw by an insidious sun,
Stared through high arcs of spray
At seas running with tuna and oyster shell;
A man at the world's edge, facing westward,
Aware that every tide is for departures;
And came home, a small Odysseus,
Having, as best I could, followed the sun.
I sit alert in the still room, hearing
The storm, knowing no end to the journey.

The chalk downs hold these rains
Like a sponge, releasing them
Through the villages in clear bournes.
Salad cresses grow there, and tiny fish,
Their world a yard of shallow pool,
Flicker among the thready roots.
The flood will be absorbed and turned
To mild uses. Five hours will bring
The sun up. We'll begin once more,
Travelling west, travelling west!